WORDO BERZERKO

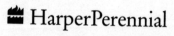

HarperPerennial

A Division of HarperCollins *Publishers*

WORDO berzerko

AN UNCOMMON DICTIONARY

RAY HAND

First Harper Perennial edition published 1990

Designed by C. Linda Dingler
Illustrations by Diana Coe

Library of Congress Cataloging-in-Publication Data

Hand, Raymond.
    Wordo berzerko / Raymond V. Hand, Jr. — 1st HarperPerennial ed.
       p.   cm.
    ISBN 0-06-096488-X (pbk.)
     1. English language—Terms and phrases—Humor.   2. Puns and punning.   3. American wit
     and humor.   I. Title.
  PN6231.W64H36   1990
  428.1'0207—dc20   89-46502

90 91 92 93 94 RRD 10 9 8 7 6 5 4 3 2 1

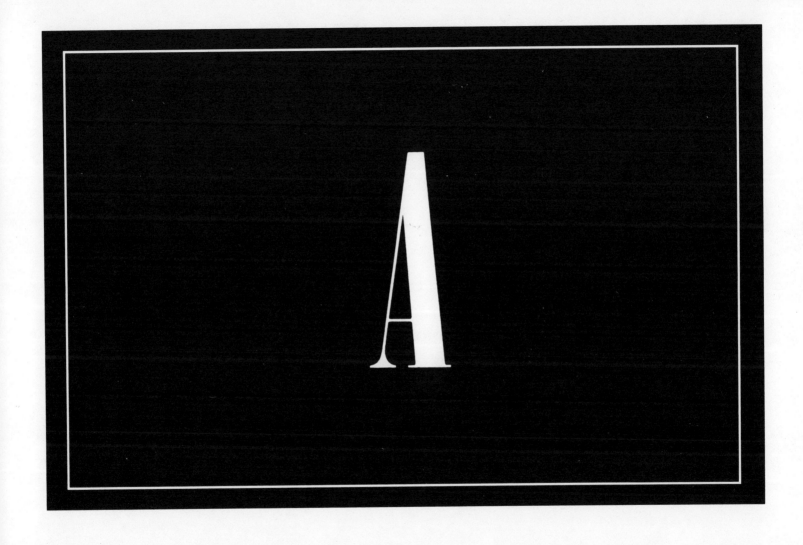

aardvark *n.* Strenuous labor.

abash *n.* A great party.

abutment *n.* An objection.

acronical *n.* A long story.

adultery *n.* Pathological condition afflicting everyone over the age of 30.

aftermath *n.* System used by IRS to calculate late-filing penalties.

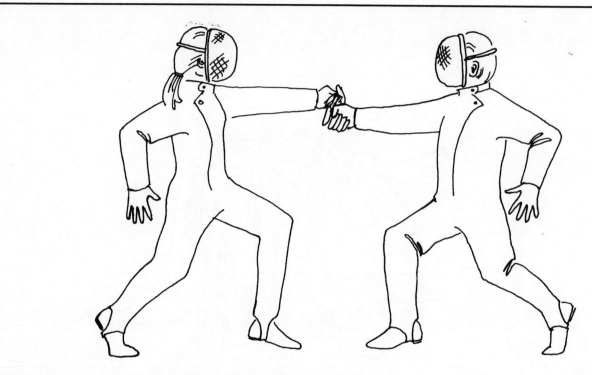

airfoil *n.* Fencing sword for hemophiliacs.

alimentary *adj.* Simple, as in,

> Watson: I say Holmes, how did you know that?
>
> Holmes: Alimentary, my dear Watson: I had a visceral intuition—a gut feeling.

apparent *n.* 1. A large, old, bossy person whose sole function is to torture young people. 2. A long-suffering innocent with an empty wallet.

appellate *n.* Small metal projectile, fired from appellate gun.

aromatic *n.* Rapid-fire bow or crossbow.

atrophy *n.* What every athlete and sportsman longs for.

awl *n.* Gold, to a Texan.

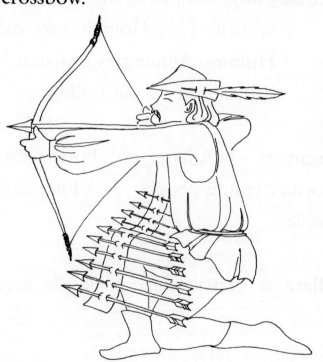

B

bacteria *n*. Lunchroom for chiropractors.

barnacle *n*. A small barn.

baroque *adj*. Emphatically fundless.

barque *n*. Sownde made by an Olde English Sheepe Dogge.

bicameral *adj.* Equipped in the fashion of the average American tourist.

bilious *adj.* Having many debts.

blunderbuss *n.* Mass transit for the hopelessly inept.

buccaneer *adj.* Very expensive variety of corn on the cob, popular among Yuppies.

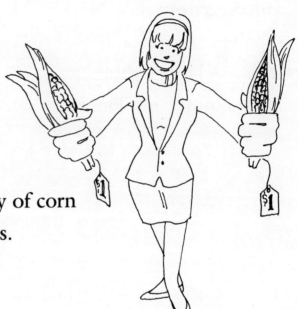

bunkhouse *n*. Place where one goes to hear nonsense. *See also* incongruous.

byte *n*. A lyttle nybble.

> **byte count** *n*. Dracula.

C

cardiac *n.* Obsessed poker player.

carpe diem *Lat. phr.* Gripe of the day.

catalyst *n.* Bovine disease,
causing the affected
animal or animals to tilt
markedly to one side.

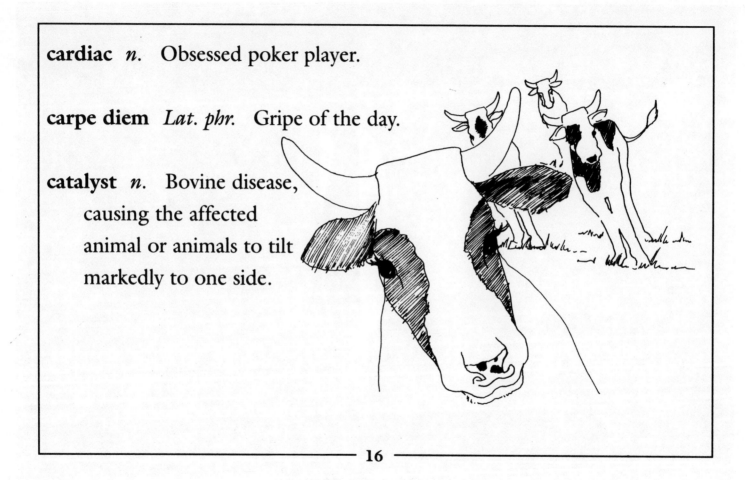

chafe *v.* Perfue with marked perfiftenfe.

chip *adj.* Not spensive.

cinnabar *n.* Saloon for the unrepentant, dive for the doomed.

collage *n.* French institute of higher education.

columbine *v.* Add up all the numbers in a column.

cranium *n.*   Place where large birds are kept.

cribbage *n.* The baby's bedroom.

critical mass *n.* Religious service for book and film reviewers.

crockery *n.* Artistic medium of the politician.

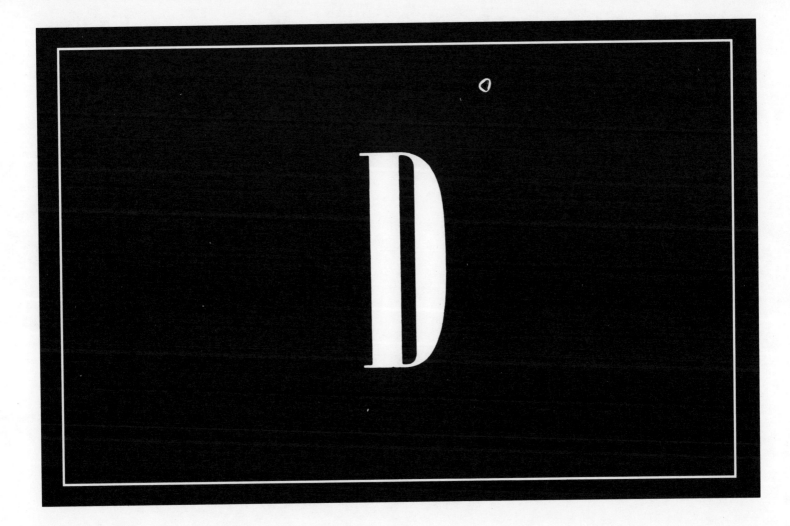

deadbeat *n.*   Jack Kerouac.

debunk *n.*   Where de cowboy sleeps,
   usually in debunk house.

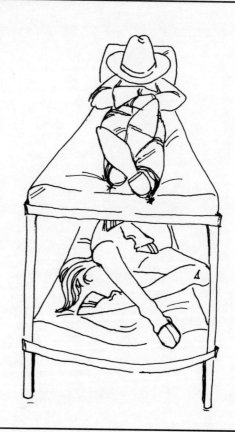

defeated *adj.* Chopped off at the ankles.

deliver *n.* What too much alcohol affects.

Democrat *n. See* **Republican.**

dense *n. pl.* The things your car ends up with, no matter how careful you are.

destabilize *v.* Take the horse out for a trot.

dethrone *n.*   Place where people do their best thinking.

discotheque *n.*   College for D.J.'s.

dismantled *adj.*   The New York Yankees
    after 1968.

dodo *n.*   Double negative with
    a head cold.

doze *n.*   Stuffed-up sniffer.

dragoon *n.*   Thug in women's attire.

E

ecru *n*. What every ship should have.

electroshock *n.* 1. A utility bill. 2. The effect of a utility bill.

étui *n.* A French tree.

exile *n.* Former island.

explication *n.*   Multiplication by the Roman numeral X.

extramural *n.*   One work of wall art too many.

extroversion *n.*   Same story, but with a different ending.

fax *n. pl.*   Truths often stranger than fixion.

fibroblast *n.*   Health food binge.

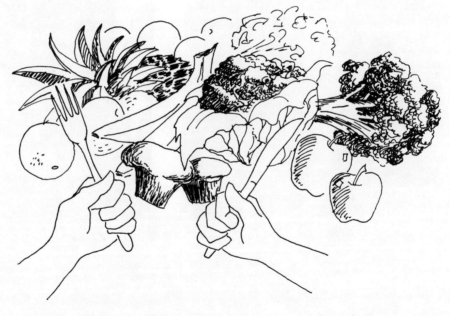

filly *adj.* Nonfenfical or even ridiculouf.

fission *n.* Outdoor sport favored by nuclear physicists.

fluorologist *n.* Floor washer with a college degree.

footnote *n.* Sole music.

forepaws *n.* Moment of silence before a golfer tees off.

forum *n.* Quartet of American Indian golfers.

G

Gaucho *n.* The Marx Brothers' South American cousin.

gladiator *adj.* How the Roman lion felt after consuming the Christian woman.

glossary *n.* Shoeshine stand.

grapeshot *n.* Vaccine for fruits.

gustatory *adj.* Very windy.

    Gustatory *n.* Where long-winded speakers go when they die.

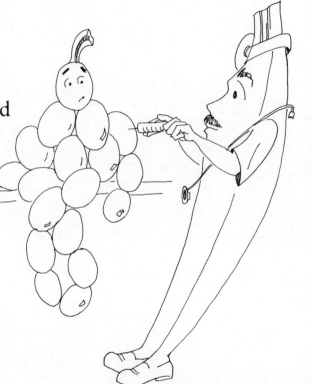

hamlet *n.*   Small pig, as in

  W. Shakespeare's soliloquy,

  "To pig out or not to pig out,

  that is indigestion."

Hebrew *n.*   Macho glass of beer.

histology *n.*   The scientific study of snakes, cats, and leaky tires.

hootenanny *n.*   An owl's nursemaid.

hundredfold *n.*   Millionaire's money clip.

impeccable *adj.* Unable to be eaten
   by a chicken.

incongruous *n.* Where most of the hot air in the U.S. is produced.

Inhibitory *n.* Place where shy people go when they die.

intense *n. pl.* Where nomads and happy campers sleep.

Iota *n.* Unpaid-for Toyota.

isobar *n.* Arctic saloon.

isolate *adj.* Delayed on account of frozen roads.

J

janissary *Obs. n.*   First month of the Ottoman calendar.

jocular *adj.*   Of or relating to sports.

K

kilohertz *n. pl.* Mortal injuries.

Kojak *n.* Second car jack — the one you have to buy after you learn (usually at night, in the winter, in a real bad section of nowhere) that the jack that came with your car isn't worth a bowlful of warm spit.

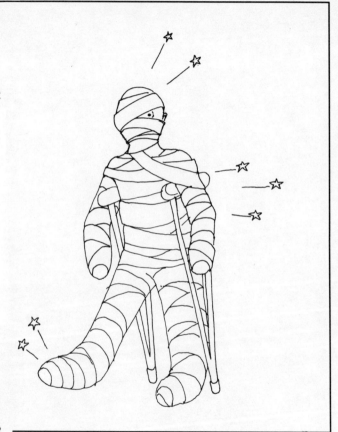

lavatory n. Volcano.

limbo n. Place where arms and legs go when they die.

Lingo *n.*   Japanese Beatle.

lingua franca *Lat. phr.*   Spaghetti with hot dogs.

locality *n.*   Quality of being nonfattening.

loft *adj.*   Mifplafed or perhapf ftolen.

M

matricide *n.*   1. The intentional killing of oneself through an overdose of sleep. 2. One who kills himself in this way.

maypole *n.*   A kind of tree, from which is drawn maypole syrup.

megahertz *n. pl.*   One million aches and pains.

Melanesia *n.*   Loss of memory in cantaloupes, honeydews, etc.

mermaid *n.*   Hydraulic wench.

microfiche *n.*   Extremely small French fish.

Micronesia *n.*   Short-term memory loss.

microwave *n.*   Form of greeting popular in Silicon Valley.

moraine *n.*   Typical springtime weather forecast.

   terminal moraine *n. phr.* Heavy rainfall afflicting commuters at train and bus stations.

motile *n.*   Hip floor covering manufactured in Detroit.

multiversity *adj.*   Knowing many poems.

nervous system *n.*   1. Communism. 2. Capitalism.

Nugatory *n.*   Where old candy bars go when they die.

oboe *n.* British tramp.

octopus *n. pl.*   A two-faced person with four heads.

olfactory *n.*   Texas petroleum refinery.

otter *adj.*   Cockney weather forecast.

P

palm oil *n.* A greenback or two, distributed where they will do the most good.

pantry *n.* 1. Health club. 2. Trouser factory.

paperweight *n.* Bureaucratic delay.

paradox *n.* 1. Very small medical group. 2. Very small marina.

pathologist *n.* Scout or tracker with a college degree.

peccary *n.* Place where the chickens eat.

penumbra *n.* 1. A writing instrument that can keep you dry. 2. An um-brella that is mightier than the sword.

perspire *adv.* How church builders calculate their construction costs.

pesticide *n.* Mercy-killing of uninvited guests, telemarketers, noisy children, nosy neighbors, and other nuisances. (In some states, pesticide is a felony. Check with your local law enforcement agency.)

polyclinic *n.* Hospital for sick parakeets.

Polynesia *n.*   Loss of memory in parrots.

porcupine *n.*   Nonkosher variety of coniferous tree.

preamble *n.*   Warm-up before a walk.

psychic *n.*   Faithful companion.

psychopath *n.*   Any urban thoroughfare during rush hour.

quarterback *n.*   Spinal ailment afflicting persons who walk around with too much change in their pockets.

quoin *n.*   Small change with a college education.

R

ragamuffin *n.*   Something to eat at a Ravi Shankar concert.

Republican *n.*   *See* **Democrat.**

rheumatism *n*. Disease
    afflicting studio apartment dwellers.

ruthless *adj*. The Boston Red Sox after 1919.

sauerbraten *Ger. n.*   Moody children.

second *n.* A nick of time.

serum *n.* One game of a series.

shrinkwrap *n.* Rhyming psychoanalytical jargon.

snorkel *n.* A cross between a snore and a chuckle.

sophisticated *adj.* Punched out.

suicide *n.*   Death by litigation.

syncopation *n.*   Ability to share the bathroom sink with others in the morning.

syntax *n.*   Revenue enhancement on human nature.

Termitory *n.* Final resting place of termites.

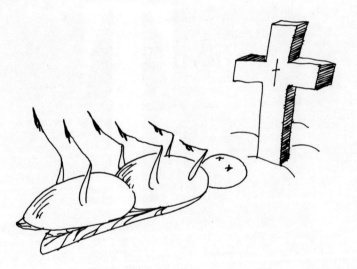

thesaurus *n.*   Giant prehistoric word, now extinct.

toucan *n.*   Two-seater outhouse.

tropical depresssion *n.*   Trouble in paradise.

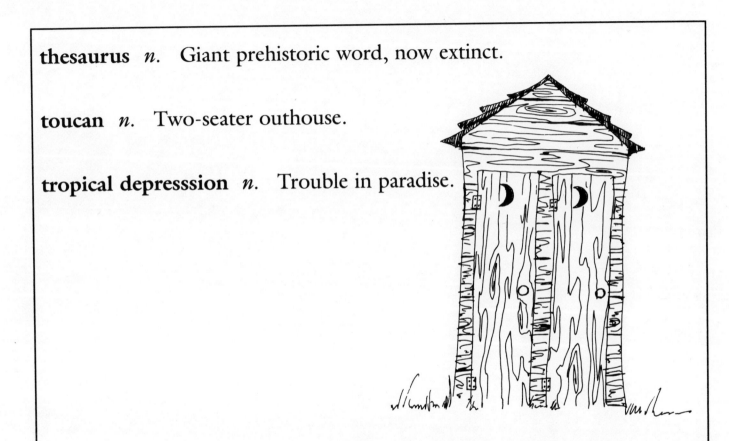

U

unicellular *adj.*   1. Having a small jail. 2. Having only one car telephone.

universe *n.*   All-purpose poem.

velocipede *n.* Very fast, many-legged creature (*Chilopoda zippo*).

versicle *n.* Eskimo poem.

viewfinder *n.* Tour guide.

Vulgate *n.* Ancient Roman political scandal.

Wedgwood *n.*   Golf club, a cross between a 9-iron and a driver.

wherewithal *n.*   Moving van.

Worcester *adj.*   Even worse than worst.

X

xat *(pr. khat) abbr.* Dead cat.

Z

zareba *n.* Zebra designed by a congressional committee.